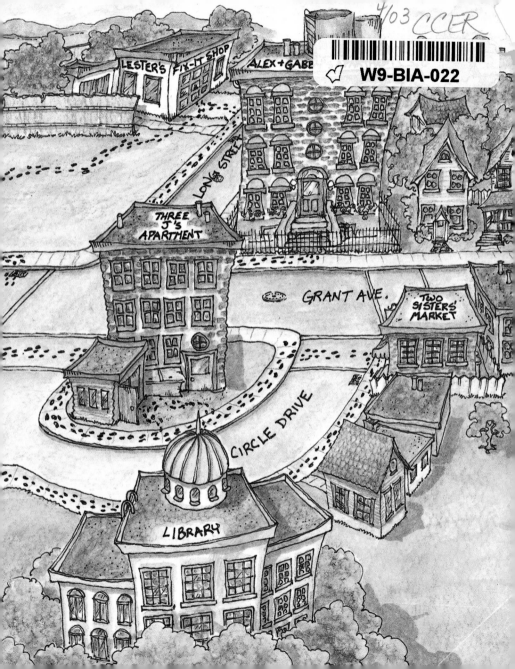

THE PET SHOW

THE CORNER KIDS

Written by Larry Dane Brimner • Illustrated by Christine Tripp

Children's Press®
A Division of Scholastic Inc.
New York • Toronto • London • Auckland • Sydney
Mexico City • New Delhi • Hong Kong
Danbury, Connecticut

For kids everywhere who love dogs
—L.D.B.

For the real Jake, my best four-legged friend.
—C.T.

Reading Consultants
Linda Cornwell
Literacy Specialist

Katharine A. Kane
Education Consultant
(Retired, San Diego County Office of Education and San Diego State University)

Library of Congress Cataloging-in-Publication Data

Brimner, Larry Dane.
 The pet show / written by Larry Dane Brimner ; illustrated by Christine Tripp.
  p. cm.
Summary: The Corner Kids learn that it takes patience to teach their dog tricks
in time for the community pet show.
 ISBN 0-516-22541-3 (lib. bdg.)   0-516-27793-6 (pbk.)
 [1. Dogs—Fiction. 2. Patience—Fiction. 3. Pet shows—Fiction.] I.Tripp, Christine, ill.
II. Title.
 PZ7.B767 Pe 2002
 [E]—dc21
                              2002005236

CHILDREN'S PRESS, AND ROOKIE CHOICES™, and associated logos are trademarks
and or registered trademarks of Grolier Publishing Co., Inc. SCHOLASTIC and associated
logos are trademarks and or registered trademarks of Scholastic Inc.
1 2 3 4 5 6 7 8 9 10 R 11 10 09 08 07 06 05 04 03 02

This book is about **patience**.

"A pet show!" said Gabby.
"Best trick wins a ribbon."

Gabby, Alex, and Three J
read the poster hanging in
the library.

5

They looked out the window at Jake. He was the dog the Corner Kids shared. The three friends called themselves the Corner Kids because they lived on opposite corners of the same street.

Alex and Three J shook their heads.

"Jake's a great dog," said Three J. "But he doesn't know any tricks."

"Except for wagging his tail," added Alex.

Gabby laughed. "It's only Monday," she said. "We have all week. We can teach him a trick."

The Corner Kids put their books in their backpacks. They went right to work teaching Jake some tricks.

Gabby tried to teach Jake to sit.
"Sit," she said.

Jake wagged his tail.

"Lie down," said Alex.

Jake wagged his tail.

"Speak," said Three J.

Jake wagged his tail.

It was the same on Tuesday and Wednesday. By Thursday, though, Jake could do other things.

Gabby said, "Roll over, Jake."
Jake sat down.

"Stay," said Alex.
Jake lay down.

"Come," said Three J.
Jake barked.

19

"He'll never get it right," Three J said.

"It takes time," said Gabby.
"Be patient with him and he'll learn."

"But we've worked every day,"
said Alex.

Gabby scratched behind Jake's ears. Then she looked serious. "Once none of us could ride a bike," she said. "But somebody took the time to teach us how."

Three J and Alex thought about that. "You're right," they said together. The Corner Kids went back to work.

On Saturday, they walked Jake to Town Park behind the library. It looked like every kid and pet in Cottonwood was there.

Mary Alice Walker showed off her pet turtle, Pete.

Ben Wong had a parrot named Chatter.

Then came Jake.

"Shake hands, Jake," Gabby said.
Jake shook hands.

"Roll over," she said.
It took a minute, then Jake rolled over.

"Look at that," said Alex. He beamed.

Three J puffed out his chest. "Patience," he said. "It works every time."

Jake was proof that it did.

31

ABOUT THE AUTHOR

Larry Dane Brimner studied literature and writing at San Diego State University and taught school for twenty years. The author of more than seventy-five books for children, many of them Children's Press titles, he enjoys meeting young readers and writers when he isn't at his computer.

ABOUT THE ILLUSTRATOR

Christine Tripp lives in Ottawa, Canada, with her husband Don; four grown children—Elizabeth, Erin, Emily, and Eric; son-in-law Jason; grandsons Brandon and Kobe; four cats; and one very large, scruffy puppy named Jake.